Passion Hunger Drive

Live Your Dreams, Not Your Fears

By Malik Champlain

Book Cover – JStreet Branding

Editor- Trisha Irving

THIS BOOK IS FOR

Jordan

Thank you

[signature]

DEDICATION

I want to thank God for making this book possible.

To my beautiful wife, family, friends, and mentors for supporting me along the way.

To my children, I want you to know that in order to reach your dreams. You have to believe that all things are possible with God.

SPECIAL THANKS

- William & Valerie Reese
- Wilberto Rodriguez
- The Siefert Family
- Peter Stathakis
- Trisha Irving

CONTENTS

FOREWORD

A person who builds structures is called an ARCHITECT. A person who builds lives is an ANKHITECT. I say this because the ANKH is an ancient Egyptian symbol (a cross with a circle on top) that represents everlasting life. I truly believe that Malik Champlain has been put on this earth to be a life builder. He has spent his whole career improving the lives of all those around him. Malik is brave enough to share his own experiences as an example or blueprint for others to follow. Regardless of age, race or economic status, there are lessons that we all can learn from his compelling story of trials and triumphs.

I first met Malik when he was interviewing for a job as a behavior technician. His responsibility was to "fix" the behavior of challenging students. It soon became clear that Malik had a different job description in mind. One that included transforming the lives of young people and adults through powerful interventions and relationship building. I remember sitting in the office for hours after school, listening to

Malik talk about his ambitious plans for the future. Right now, you have an opportunity to read about what it took for Malik to turn his dreams into a reality. You will also see how he applied the principles of Passion, Hunger and Drive in his own life in order to become the father, brother, son, leader, and friend that he is today.

Malik has given motivational speeches to my students at the Journalism and Media Academy in Hartford, Connecticut as well as other schools around the country. The feedback that my students consistently share is that Mr. Champlain "Keeps It Real." Malik has lived up to his reputation of telling the truth about his past and leaves the reader with the desire to learn even more. I highly recommend *Passion Hunger Drive- Live Your Dreams Not Your Fears* to everyone, especially educators who are interested in inspiring their students with a real example of strength and determination.

Peace,

Leonard Epps, Principal

Introduction

CEO "Chief Empowerment Officer"
Malik Champlain

I wasn't meant to be homeless--I wasn't meant not to *have*. I went from being labeled Special Ed to earning my Master's Degree; I went from being speechless to being a motivational speaker, from being homeless to being a homeowner

For me, it's just about righting the wrongs and not letting someone else tell my story. I'm trying to give back to my community because success shouldn't be a secret ---- it's not like a member's only club. It's this thing that no matter who you are adult or child: Passion, Hunger, and Drive is in all of us! It's about bringing that greatness out of you: finding what makes you really tick or what will make you get up in the morning. It is about finding what will make you rise and grind everyday. What is it that will make you work all night and still wake up at 3 or 4 in the morning to achieve your dreams?

I don't even sleep anymore; I swear I just have visions about what's going to happen in my future. When you dream, are you thinking about a fantasy that won't happen or are you dreaming about a vision that is going to become a reality?

Why did I write this book?

I wrote this book because I wanted to empower people who are like me -- who are seen as the underdog, who were told that they would be nothing. I'm here to tell you that right now, today, this moment is your moment; this time is your time to be whoever YOU want to be, to live your dreams and not your fears, to ignore the haters and succeed anyways. I want to speak life into people and help them understand that success is a part of their reality.

My objective is to motivate the unmotivated, to inspire the people who need to be inspired. I want to push people from average to good, from good to great, from great to unstoppable! There is something inside of me that is driven to give to people that which people tried to take and steal from me. I'm living proof of the American Dream. I'm living proof that no matter what people have done or will do to you, that as long as you don't let them destroy you, as long as you bend-- you will never BREAK. First you survive, and once you survive you can thrive.

Now I want you to trust me, you're going to do an empowerment exercise.

I want you to speak these words into existence:

I have Passion, I have Hunger, I have Drive;

I am Powerful, I am Fearless, I am Unstoppable,

I am Alive, I am Amazing, I am a Champion,

I am Strong, I will Live my Dreams and Face my FEARS!

Repeat 2x or until you believe it!

Pay attention! Your Dreams Are Possible!

I know that you have a dream deep inside of you. I'm talking about a dream that you didn't tell anyone else, I mean you don't even say it out loud to yourself because it sounds that crazy or impossible. I want to tell you that dream that you're holding on to is POSSIBLE!! It is beyond possible. So don't make the biggest mistake of your life by dismissing this dream. I actually want you to have the type of imagination where you dream your biggest and wildest dreams. And then I need for you to have the courage to open your eyes and work towards that dream until it is a reality.

In order to make your dreams a reality you have to care about every minute of your day. There are too many people that are doing stuff that is unproductive. I mean they allow their wants to dictate their lives instead of their needs. Watching TV, playing video games, eating fast food, and sleeping in - these are all wants and luxuries. You see, if you have a dream that you have not achieved yet, you don't deserve your wants until you satisfy your needs. Accomplishing your dreams comes down to *Priorities.* Ask yourself, *what are your priorities?* and how bad do you want to attain this goal or dream that you have?

I need for you to understand the dream is free but the hustle is sold separately. So you can tell people over and over again about how you have these big dreams but you have to be willing to lose sleep, to work hard, and to sacrifice. Think about those dreams: that college admission, that job promotion, that start-up business, that spot on the team.

It is all possible; but first you have to be willing to be the first up and the last to go to sleep, not just one day or two days a week. I mean *every day*! You have to make a habit of doing what other people don't want to do. This means when others are sleeping you're grinding, when others are partying you're grinding, when others quit, you just keep on grinding! Because that is how winning is done, that is how dreams are built. So regardless of your situation, every day you wake up I need you to Rise and GRIND!

I'm starting off this book telling you that your dreams are possible and now I want to ask you a question: *what is the distance between your dreams and your reality? I mean, what will push you to make your dreams come true?*

I believe this is the age-old question that every winner that hasn't won yet has asked themselves. I believe that is what you are-- a winner who just hasn't won yet. Don't let the fact that your dreams are not currently present overwhelm you. If you have been working towards a dream, keep on fighting! Your dream is not dead, it is alive! Your dream has not left you, it is right on time! Your dream is coming it's just not in season yet!

I have three words that will change the way you think about life, which will change the decisions you make in life, which will change the way you attack your life. I'm telling you losing is for losers and that is not you. Failing is for failures and that is not you. Pity is for victims and that will no longer be you. It's time to start living your true life with these three words: **Passion, Hunger, and Drive**. Those words will take your life from good to great, great to unstoppable--and even phenomenal.

Chapter 1- Passion

If you're scared to take chances you'll never have the answers.

-Nas

If you define the word "passion" in Webster's dictionary the definition reads: *a strong feeling of enthusiasm or excitement for something or about doing something.* When I look at this definition, I think that in order for someone to have passion they must first know what it is that makes them have "enthusiasm" or "excitement".

This got me thinking that everyone who reads this book needs to get M.A.D. and I mean as soon as possible. When I write M.A.D. I mean everyone has to "Make A Decision" on who they want to be and what they want to pursue. Throughout my life I noticed that the most successful people I know always knew exactly what they did and did not want in life.

My own understanding of the word "passion" considers the clarity or F.O.C.U.S (Following One Course Until Success) of your dreams. I believe this idea of F.O.C.U.S. is a key to success, figure out that one course of action and keep grinding until it becomes a reality. In order to be successful in life, you have to put some skin in the game and be willing to be fully committed to your "Plan A". I challenge you to make a decision in your life to pursue that one dream that contains your hopes and goals and never look back.

A few years ago, I came across this quotation by Howard Thurman that states, "Don't ask what the world needs, instead ask what makes you come alive and go do that, because what the world needs is people who have come alive." When I think about this quote, it embodies everything that I strive to accomplish in life.

I'm not trying to figure out what the next gimmick is or the next hot new fad. Instead, from the moment I read this quotation, I made a decision to follow my dreams and never settle until I find the things that make me come alive. I want you to ask yourself: *what makes you come alive*? What are you passionate about? What will you happily do every day for free? You might be asking yourself, how do I know if I've found my passion? Or, how do I determine what makes me come alive? From experience, I can tell you in life there are a lot of things that people have to force themselves to do: getting up for work, going to the gym, and maintaining a diet, etc.

The great thing about finding your focus and what makes you come alive is that once you find your passion your expectations changes. I mean once you understand your true worth you will never let anyone short change you again. For example, the second I felt completely alive as a public speaker, completely alive having my own business, completely alive owning my own home, I had to *chase* that feeling. These are the expectations that I maintain for myself because that is now what living is to me. I refuse to go backwards.

Passion makes life worth living, and I will never be interested in knowing what it is like to live without it. In my years of education and in various jobs, I have seen my fair share of people who go through life without passion, and I feel sorry for them. When I walk into some classrooms or boardrooms, it's like a zombie scene from "The Walking Dead". I see people who dread going to work or school and they rush back home to their TV or video games, just to wake up and do it again.

There is so much you can gain if you stop *going through* life and start *getting from* life. Learn from your failures, face your fears, laugh until you cry, and work extremely hard at everything you do. Live with passion, focus, and appreciate the little things in life. Never settle for anything less than your best, and truly figure out what makes you come ALIVE!

Reflection

1. What makes you come ALIVE?

2. List several dreams that you want to achieve in life.

3. Write down what you think is stopping you from achieving your dreams.

Chapter 2 – Bad Night

"Good dude, bad night, right place, wrong time.
In the blink of an eye, his whole life changed"
-Kanye West

One night, when I was 16 years old, the phone rang. It was my brother-- well actually it was my friend "Dee" (but he is like a brother to me). Now earlier in the day he had asked me to go to this party on the other side of town. I told him not to go because dudes from that side of town *did not like us*. It was a territorial thing. I picked up the phone and Dee said, "You got to come and get me, there are some guys outside and I don't know if they have weapons, and I think they want to jump me."

At this point in time, the only thing I was thinking is one of my best friends is in a situation where he might get hurt. It didn't matter that I just made the basketball team. It didn't matter that I just started to get my grades together. It didn't matter that I just started believing that college was for me. At that point in time, the only thing I was thinking about was the loyalty I had for my friend.

Before I hung up the phone I told him, "I'm coming" and "be safe until I get there". I knew what I had to do. I don't know if you have these types of friends, but I call these my ride or die homies. You know--- the dudes from the block who are actually "Real Gangsters", they don't just look like them. These are not the dudes that you would invite over for Sunday Dinner, but they are always down to participate if there is conflict involved. After I called, it took them no more than 10 minutes to come pick me up.

We were driving in this late model Toyota Camry, there were four of us. I sat in the back.

On the way over there, my mind kept racing: *Were we going to get there in time to protect him and have his back?* I remember clearly how dark the car was as we drove; there was a fleeting flash of light every few seconds from passing the street lamps. Then, in the darkness, I felt something heavy fall on my lap. At the time I didn't know what it was, but as I unwrapped the bandana around it I felt the metal and knew it was a gun. As I looked up, I knew they could see the surprise in my eyes. I just didn't want them to see the fear. My heart started to race and then someone said, "You ready?", and I replied, "Yeah I'm ready for whatever".

When we pulled up, I saw a group of guys outside the building where Dee was. I got out the car and tucked the gun in my waistband, pulling my shirt over it. I looked at the top of the stairs and saw my boy Dee.

As I walked to the front of the car, I noticed another guy walked towards us with his hands in his shirt. He asks, "What's up?" and then pulls his shirt up slightly to flash his piece—his gun. Then I said, "It's Whatever." and I pull up my shirt and flash the gun I had. At this point, my heart is racing, everything is escalating too fast, I don't have time to think and I heard Dee loudly yell, "Malik!!" I whip my head around as I hear the two scariest noises of my life: "*pap pap*" two gunshots go off. For some reason, I could only just close my eyes. From that moment on, everything changed.

Reflection

Did I deal with this situation the correct way? Why or why not?

How could this situation been handled differently?

Chapter 3- Tough Times

"All that I got is you
and I'm so thankful I made it through"
-Mary J Blige

When it comes to my life, the theme might be, "tough times don't last, tough people do". I have learned first-hand from experience that this is true, and a lot of how I learned that lesson came from my mother.

My mother is the toughest person I know. She had me at seventeen in Brooklyn, NY back in 1985. Plenty of people told my mother that it was a mistake to have me, and that she was better off to have an abortion than ruin her life with a child. Due to her pregnancy, she couldn't go back and complete the 12th grade, which meant she couldn't get a high school diploma.

During this time, the odds were stacked even higher against her; however, my mother told me she always lived by that statement, "Tough times don't last, tough people do".

When I was a child, my mother and grandmother had no problem holding me to high expectations. Even though I grew up in a low-income neighborhood with drug dealers on every corner and gangs on every block, they always made it a point to tell me that I could be anything I wanted to be in this world.

My grandmother would remind me of that fact even though I couldn't physically leave the metal fence around our brownstone in Brooklyn because it was too dangerous. My dreams didn't live right outside my windows or my fence, but they did live inside of my books and my imagination. I spent a lot of hours sitting on my front steps flipping through pages of picture books imagining myself traveling the world.

Beyond my geographical barriers, I also struggled with my own perceptions of physical barriers as well. I didn't say my first word until I was four years old. The doctors and psychologists didn't know what was wrong with my speaking; however, when I did finally start to speak, I spoke with a stutter.

It wasn't until I moved to Connecticut from New York, and I went swimming for the first time that we knew the problem was actually physical. When I got out the pool, I told my mother that my ears still felt like they were under water and I had problems hearing. She brought me to the doctor and they found out I had fluid in my ears that needed to be drained and I needed surgery to implant hearing tubes. This problem with my ears that caused my stuttering would later cause me a lot of trouble academically and socially.

During this time, I remember all of the trips my mother took to the Capitol building in Connecticut, fighting for the State to pay for my speech therapist. The school I went to didn't provide one at first.

One day, I remember looking at my mom in the car: she was tired, frustrated, and looked like she had been crying. After all, my mother had been driving once or twice a week for an hour each way to the Capitol building to fight for me.

I remember telling her "Maybe we should just give up, I'll be ok." She quickly turned and looked me in my eyes and said, "If you want something you have to fight for it, nobody is going to give you anything in life for free."

Those were some powerful words and even at my young age I kind of understood what she meant. I remember how hard my mother fought until we got the money for the speech services. Her level of resilience and determination would later serve as critical models to me as I fought my own struggles.

During my childhood, it continued to feel like my mind and body were playing tricks on me. Throughout grade school,

I continued to have a very bad stuttering problem. I could hear the voice in my head saying the words exactly as they were supposed to sound. Something just kept going wrong when I tried to speak. Typically, my attempts to speak would follow with other kids laughing and teasing me. At this age, I was an easy target for bullies and I quickly learned to say little to nothing in class.

I mostly hated Thursdays at this one school I went to. Every week on this day, the reading teacher came in. She would have all the students that didn't read very well sit in the front and this would be prior to lunch and recess. She would have us take turns reading out loud to the class. As I waited for my turn, I could hear the other students laughing and making fun of the students that couldn't read well before me. My fear of stuttering and being teased intensified as it got closer and closer to my turn. When it was finally my turn, I started to refuse to read every week. I lost a lot of recess time for not reading to the class but things would soon change.

Reflection

1. Explain a time you were teased in school? How has that shaped your life today?

2. Where do you see yourself in 5 years? Describe what that looks like?

3. If you could travel anywhere in the world where would you go? And why?

Chapter 4 - The Secret

"Now all the teachers couldn't reach me
And my momma couldn't beat me
Hard enough to match the pain of my pops not seeing me"
-Jay Z

I grew up moving a lot living with my mother, grandmother, and my father when he wasn't in jail. By the time I was eight years old, I already had my PHD--but it was in Pain, Hatred, and Defiance. It was at this age in my life when my attitude changed dramatically, especially when I found out that there had been a secret that everyone was keeping from me.

In the spring of 1993, I had just turned 8 years old, and the highlight of that year was my father coming home from jail. I remember the day he was released so vividly, and it has always been the happiest day of my childhood.

We were living in Willimantic, CT in what was known as "The Heights". In the early 90's, this place was filled with drug dealers, drug users, and gang bangers. What I hated the most about living there was that we had the bottom tenant apartment with all the roaches, ants, and those "pincher bugs". During this time, we didn't have a car and my mother was working part time trying to juggle the bills. On the weekdays, school provided breakfast and lunch, but on the weekend if I didn't wake up early enough to meet the white van with the free lunch bags filled with peanut butter and jelly sandwiches, a milk box, and a box of raisins, my brother and I probably didn't eat until dinner.

One day, I was down the street with my friends playing "Red Light, Green Light, 1,2,3". I was standing completely still so I wouldn't get called out when I heard my mother yell for me. I could have been 5 blocks away and I still would have heard my mother's call. I came home racing, hoping I wasn't in trouble. I kept running through the list in my mind, "Well I made my bed, washed the dishes and...ooooh I know I didn't take out the trash". As I got home, I knocked on the door with my hand out expecting the same lecture accompanied with a bag of garbage to take out. Instead, I saw my father.

I couldn't believe it! I was so overwhelmed with emotion that I instantly burst into tears of joy. He had just finished doing a little more than three years in prison. During that time we never went to visit him because my mother always said she never wanted her sons to see the inside of a penitentiary. I prayed night after night when he was gone for him to come home. At one point, I felt like I started to forget what his face looked like, and I would carry this picture of me and him in a red metal frame to remind myself. This was the happiest day of my life!

I walked back outside and my friends ran up to me asking, "Yo, what happened?" I replied, "MY DAD IS HOME!!"

All of a sudden, I remember us in a new, super-clean apartment living in Norwich, CT. I knew it was clean because I was allowed to lay on the rug. It was such an awesome rug; it was baby-blue and it felt so good on my skin.

I was on cloud nine for months after my dad came home from prison, but this all came to a big crash toward the end of summer.

Over the summer, most of my friends all went to the local YMCA's Camp Anderson to stay busy and out of trouble. I would normally get dropped off and picked up by the school bus to camp. One day, however, I was running late so my dad dropped me off at the YMCA with the other kids waiting on the bus to take us to camp.

On the bus ride to camp, all of my friends kept asking me if my dad was my *real dad*, I was like, "Yea of course he is." The other kids laughed, especially the older kids, and stated that he couldn't be my dad because he was light skinned and I was dark. At the time, I didn't think much of it because my family came in all shades and sizes. However, by the end of the day, what the kids said to me on the bus took its toll and confused me. I felt resolved knowing that I knew if I asked my mom she would tell me the truth.

Later in the afternoon, my mother picked me up from the YMCA. I sat in the back and started to yell over the music a few times to get my mother's attention. She turned down the music and said, "Yes, Malik" I replied, "These kids on the bus keep telling me that dad isn't my real dad because we don't look alike, and then I told them about how you and my aunt don't look alike and you guys are sister's and…"

My mother said, "Malik" and first she pulled over and then gave me this stare from the rear view mirror. I could see her eyes start to tear up and I said, "What mommy?" She replied, "Dad is not your REAL father, but it doesn't mean that he doesn't love you like you are his son". All I could say was, "Stop lying! Stop lying! Dad is my father!" as I grabbed my backpack and stuffed it in my face. I started crying as loud as I possibly could into the backpack. My mother reached over and rubbed my back and repeatedly told me she was "sorry".

A few minutes later, like many times before, my mother directed me to look at her and she said, "Your biological father left us soon after you were born and your "Dad" has been in our lives ever since taking care of us the best way he knows how and he treats you like you are his own blood." This was a

29

lot to take in at 8 years old, but the hardest part was when my mom made me promise not to mention it to anyone, especially not my "Dad".

Reflection

1. What is your relationship with your father?

2. Write down a time when you felt like you didn't fit in.

Chapter 5 – Killing Me Softly

"You're my little secret, And that's how we should keep it. We should never let 'em know, Never let it show."

-Xscape

After that car ride with my mother, I kept that secret. I carried the burden, but I crumbled inside. I bottled up every emotion, but it began to surface in the form of physical aggression and destructive behavior at home and in the classroom. I found myself getting in trouble all the time in school. I punched holes in walls and doors. I was so angry and it never seemed to go away. I felt close to worthless: *why didn't my father want to be in my life?*

It felt even worse because I didn't have anyone to talk to about what was going on with me on the inside. My defiant behavior didn't change because no punishment could hurt or affect me like the pain of not having my biological father in my life. Looking back, this bad behavior, as everyone saw it, was actually a cry for help, but no one was listening.

Antwone Fisher's poem, entitled <u>Who Will Cry for the</u>
<u>Little Boy</u> asks:

> *"Who will cry for the little boy?*
> *A good boy he tried to be*
> *Who will cry for the little boy?*
> *Who cries inside of me."*

I heard this poem much later in my life, but it reflected
so well how I felt as an 8 year old. I was crushed by the news
that my biological father didn't want to be in my life.

To make matters worse, I would be in public with my
family and people would recognize my siblings as their kids
then ask if I was their nephew or family friend and not their
son. Those situations would kill me on the inside, because I
was already carrying the heavy burden of the secret of my
father on my shoulders. This was a lot for a boy who just
wanted to fit in and wanted for his father to love him.

My mother is Native American and my "dad"---I guess
you would call him my "step dad" — (it even feels weird calling
him that) was Puerto Rican. This made things difficult for me,
because I lived in a family where no one resembled me. My
skin was a lot darker, my hair a lot nappier, and I just felt like I
didn't fit in.

On some nights, I would tell myself that my mother was
lying to me. My father simply did not know where I was and

would come through the front door saying that he had been looking for me for a long time. He'd tell me that he loved me and everything would be okay!

But he never came, and that never happened.

"I remember asking my mother why my father didn't want me. And she looked me in my eyes and said, "Baby you're a blessing and you come from me. I named you Malik, which is a name for a King.

Even though your father is not around, never doubt yourself. Look every man in the eye and always hold your head up high."

-Malik Champlain

Reflection

I am

_____

(Two features about you)

I wonder

_____

(Something you contemplate about a lot)

I hear

_____

(What do you hear when you close your eyes)

I see

_____

(Write down what you see in your dreams)

I want

_____

(A wish you have)

I feel

_____

(A emotion you have deep inside you)

I worry

_____

(Something that troubles you)

I cry

_____

(Something that makes you sad)

I say

_____

(Something you believe in)

Chapter 6 - The Mirror

"It's not about the cards you're dealt, but how you play the hand."

- Randy Pausch

From the time I was eight when my mother told me that secret until I was old enough to understand my father wasn't going to come looking for me, I felt like I was the victim. I felt like my father, my family, the world — everyone-- owed me something because my life wasn't fair.

I felt worthless, because I was looking at myself through his eyes, instead of through the eyes of those who loved me: my mother, my brothers, and my *real father, the man who was raising me.*

I cradled this secret and it felt like I was walking around with a weight vest that got heavier each day, week, month, and year. I need you to understand: It is not your burden to carry; it is not your responsibility. If you're reading this, regardless of your age, I'm giving you permission to "LET IT GO!" Let go of the pain, let go of the anger, let go of the revenge, let go of all the missed opportunities, just let it go! I know it will not be easy.

I remember that eventually there came a time in my life when I wanted to forgive my father, but I couldn't. I had held on to that anger for so long it felt like a part of me. I just didn't know how not to be angry. Then, one day, I woke up and decided that this pain was eating me up on the inside, and I wasn't going to let it any more.

At 13, I stopped feeling bad for myself and started coming to grips with my own reality which was:

Yes, my biological father left me.

Yes, I have a speech impediment.

Yes, I come from a low-income family.

But these weren't good enough reasons to give up on myself. Instead of giving up and feeling bad for myself, I then decided to embrace my personal struggles. I was tired of looking in the mirror and not liking what looked back at me.

I made the decision to lock myself in the bathroom and stare in the mirror until I liked what I was looking at. I started looking at myself and *really* looking for the first time in my life. I literally was in a staring contest with myself-- or at least it felt that way. A couple of minutes felt like hours. I felt my mind thinking again about how worthless I was and this caused me to get angry with myself. The angrier I got, the more the tears started to run down my face. I felt like I went through every range of emotion. I just kept staring in the mirror--I refused to look away. I stared until the tears dried up and my eyes cleared.

I told myself, "Malik he's not walking through those doors, he's not coming here to save you. You have to prove to him and to everybody else that they are wrong about you. That you will achieve greatness, that you will be successful even though people will laugh at you about being placed into special education classes. Even though people have doubted you, you're going to promise yourself to use all this pain and anger you have built up inside to be even more successful, more amazing, more phenomenal!"

Here's the thing. I know that many of you have a similar story. Your life is not fair, things are hard, and it is a struggle to just survive sometimes, never mind making the effort to chase your dreams.

My challenge to you is to "Love Yourz" like the J. Cole song, there is not a life that's better than yours, because "IT'S YOUR'S!" All the money, success, or fame in the world will not be worth it if you don't first have love for yourself. "What will it profit anyone if they gain the whole world, yet lose their soul?"

I challenge you to go to your bathroom at home, look in the mirror, and first accept who you truly are. Do this by really looking at and analyzing yourself; tell yourself every little thing you believe you are good, great, and extraordinary at! Lastly, leave that mirror dedicated to live for what matters most important in your life.

Reflection

1. List all the reason that you CAN achieve your dreams/goals.

2. When you look in the mirror what do you see?

3. Write down a time in your life when you had to overcome an obstacle.

Chapter 7 – Hunger

"There's no way I can pay you back.
But the plan is to show you that I understand
You are appreciated"
– Tupac Shakur

I once heard that if you know your "WHY", you can overcome any "HOW". This stuck with me because before I found my Passion Hunger and Drive, I had Pain, Hatred, and Destruction. I blamed a lot of people for the way my life was going and the disadvantages. This made me angry, but most of all this made me a VICTIM. Yes, I was a victim to what everyone else did or didn't do for me. I told myself that I could never be successful: my father wasn't around, I was living in section 8 housing, I was placed in special education classes, and the kids at school made fun of me for my speech impediment.

Then I remembered all of the nights that I saw my mother come home tired from work. She came home just to take a quick nap and then got up and went to her second job or to school. I remember my mother giving me her lunch money for the week, so I could go on my school field trip. I remember all of the nights she read a book with me and told me I was special even though I personally didn't feel that way.

At this time, my mother was my "WHY". I saw how hard she had it, the odds she was up against, and she never complained or gave excuses. My GRIND and HUSTLE to be great and successful in life started from looking at my mother struggle.

I started telling myself that one day, she will not have to work this hard to survive. My mother set the blueprint for my *hunger* because she embodied it herself. She went from cleaning toilets to working her way up the corporate ladder to being an Information Systems Manager in the IT Department at Foxwoods Casino. My mother is the living example that a rose can truthfully rise from the concrete. All she needed was her PHD....PASSION, HUNGER and DRIVE.

Now, I want you to think about your "WHY", because that is what's going to push you when you're feeling sick and tired. Your WHY is what will stop you from quitting, or making excuses for yourself. Your WHY is what will get you up early in the morning to chase a dream no one else can see, but you and it will keep you going until late at night. Your WHY will be the deciding factor on whether you win or lose, succeed or fail, step up or back down. I see a warrior in you but before you go to battle remember WHY you started, what woke you up this morning, and WHY failure is not an option!

Reflection

1. Write down all the people that have supported and encouraged your personal success?

2. What's your WHY?

Chapter 8 - Through Struggle Comes Success

"Sky is the limit and you know that you can have what you want, be what you want."
-Notorious B.I.G.

When I was 13 years old, I made a decision that would change my life. Up to this time, I had been speaking with a serious speech impediment. This caused me to be very quiet, shy, and an easy target for bullies. At this age, anything that made you stand out was an easy target for a bully to make fun of you. I remember bullies picking on me for not being able to complete my words, and other kids would laugh because they didn't want to be bullied themselves. It was easy to make fun of the kid who didn't say much.

I would come home at night and ask my mother why the other kids would make fun of me. She would fill me up with words of encouragement and tell me that if people only knew me, they would love me. I love my mother for that toughness one minute and the next making you feel like you are loved beyond measure.

Now that I was 13, I was done feeling bad for myself. I knew that in order to deal with my fear of speaking – the fear which fueled my stuttering problem – I had to attack it head on. So I decided that I was going to take my collection of *Goosebumps* books by R.L. Stein and read them out loud. I sat in the living room and I read those *Goosebumps* books out loud to myself all summer. I kept reading and reading and reading until I got cotton-mouth. It was not easy; I was fighting through words. I ripped pages out. But, no matter what kind of day I had, "I NEVER QUIT".

It wasn't magic, but by the end of the summer I felt a lot more comfortable speaking out loud. I graduated from speaking to stuffed animals, to my younger brothers, and even to a few friends. I even taught myself a few tricks to get through a word I was stuck on; I snapped my fingers, slapped my leg, and stomped on the floor, but I found that the most important strategy was to control my breathing. These would be the beginning stages to helping me Live my Dreams and not my Fears!

Life isn't fair and it surely isn't easy; however, believing in yourself is vital to your success. Up until this point in my life, I felt like I wasn't successful at anything. I had allowed the negative things people said about me to become my reality. I was lacking the confidence to make any changes in my life.

But there was always a small voice in my head that told me I was meant to be more and all I had to do was listen to it. I had to stop listening to the adults that told me that college wasn't an option; I had to stop listening to the kids that told me I would be a nobody. I decided to start believing in myself and in my dreams. After getting myself in the right mindset to be successful, I won half the battle and the rest relied on me showing up everyday willing to put in the work necessary for success. I got to the point where I was sick and tired of being bullied and being the victim. Then I told myself that I couldn't control what other people would do or say, but I could work on improving myself.

Reflection

1. Write down five positive things about yourself.

2. What is stopping you from living your dreams?

Chapter 9 - Turn Your Dreams Into Reality

"Dream chaser, keep chasin'
Grind will turn into your shine, be patient"
-Meek Mill

Dreams are not meant to stay just dreams. We are supposed to manifest our dreams into reality. This is why dreaming big is so important, because too many people dream of things that are easily accomplished or achieved. A lot of dreams are really just visions of the future. If we believe we can have them and work towards these dreams, they will eventually come to be the past.

I grew up with a speech impediment and still have it to this day. However, as a child, I dreamed of not having a speech impediment. At least once a week, I had this recurring dream where I walked onto a big stage with giant spotlights shining on me, and the only thing I could hear was the roar of the crowd as I headed to the podium to give a speech.

I bring this up because, if I had listened to reality, I would have remained the kid that people laughed at. I would have doubted my ability to speak publicly for the rest of my life. Instead, I believed that my dream was my reality, and that I had to work at achieving my dream, regardless of the obstacles and struggles that were ahead of me.

#DREAMCHASING

Dream, Dream, Dream, Dream Chasing

Dream, Dream, Dream, Dream Chasing

Dream, Dream, Dream, Dream Chasing

Life is a gift, so I hope you're not wasting!

My mother had me at 17 out running the streets.

Had to hold me close because we couldn't afford the heat.

My real father didn't want me said he isn't going to take it.

Even family turned their back like we aren't gonna make it.

Momma always loved me, daddy hide and ran.

Looked in the mirror couldn't understand I was just a boy.

Yea trying to be a man.

I was just a boy but I had to help feed the fam.

- Malik Champlain

Reflection

1. Write down your BIGGEST DREAM. Describe what it looks, feels, sounds, and smells like.

2. Write down all the steps it takes to make your dream a reality.

Chapter 10 - Don't Do Your Best, Do Whatever It Takes

"Look If you had one shot or one opportunity to seize everything you ever wanted, in one moment, would you capture it or just let it slip?"
-Eminem

W.I.T. stands for "Whatever It Takes". I will be the first to tell you that "YOUR BEST?" isn't good enough if you are waking up to strive for greatness. There are going to be some goals in life where your best isn't going to cut it and you will have to do "Whatever it takes". As humans we all have limitations, but the worst thing in life is not falling short of a big dream; the worst thing is dreaming too small and actually achieving it. Everyday WE put limitations on ourselves due to doubt, fear, and negative self talk! WE sometimes talk ourselves out of growing, succeeding, and reaching the next level in life.

When I was a sophomore in high school I tried out for the boy's basketball team at my school -- Norwich Free Academy (NFA) the home of the Wildcats. To give you some background, we had the #1 player in the state, Mark Jones, and another stand out player in Kenny Jones. That year's team would later go to the state championship game, and both Mark and Kenny would receive scholarships to play college basketball.

Up until that point in my life, I wasn't allowed to play sports except for a short stint with 8th grade football. The reason I couldn't play was due to the fact that I had to watch over my little brothers and we couldn't afford a babysitter. Growing up in my family, we understood that family was all that you had, and when times are tough we stick together "No matter what". Yes, I wanted to go have fun after school with my friends and Yes I wanted to play sports especially in high school. However, I understood that when it comes to family, you sometimes have to sacrifice for the ones you love.

Then right before basketball season started my mother got a new job that made more money and she let me try out for the basketball team. The only problem was that I was out of shape and not that good of a basketball player, but, in my mind, I thought I could walk into the gym and make the team without being in shape or giving maximum effort. After the coach ran us into the ground over the course of three days, I got cut on the last day of tryouts. I remember walking into the head coach's office and he looked me in my eyes and told me, "Malik you're not in good enough shape to play on the team and you need to work on your basketball skills". I said, "I'm better than half the players on the court!" He replied, "You didn't work hard enough over the last three days to show me that".

I was crushed. That night I went home and I put my face in my pillow and I cried in my room for hours until my mother came in. I told her what happened, expecting some sympathy or maybe a hug, but instead she said, "What are you crying for?" Shocked, I said, "huh?" She said, "You think you're the only one that got knocked down in life? Well, son, here is the truth: life is tough, and I raised you better than to sit around here feeling bad for yourself. You need to get out there and get better in basketball and find a way to get on that team." And I replied, "Mom, how am I going to get on the team? The coach does not think I'm good enough?" Then she said the words I needed to hear: "You need to do WHATEVER IT TAKES!"

I bring up this story for two reasons: one, to show you another reason why my mother is my WHY and my biggest cheerleader, and two, to give you an example of how changing your mindset can change your life. After this talk, I immediately stopped feeling bad for myself and started doing all the work that was necessary to try and make the team the following year. I woke up at 5 am to work out and get up shots before school, went directly to the weight room after school instead of hanging out with my friends, and spent my weekend nights at the basketball court shooting until the lights went out instead of partying. I was willing to do whatever it took to achieve my goal because it wasn't just about making the team.

Prior to being cut from the basketball team, I never really had a passion for anything in my life and that reflected in my work ethic. But now I knew I had to raise my game on the court, from average to good and from good to great.

That summer, I taped three notes for myself to read every day on my bathroom mirror. They said,

"You're not good enough"

"You didn't work hard enough"

"Whatever it takes!"

Prior to this I never worked harder for anything in my life. This was the first time I ever put 100% percent into something and knew from the beginning that I wouldn't quit. I went from a boy who was interested in making the basketball team to a young man who was committed, dedicated, and driven.

The following school year I went out for the team but I had a completely different mindset. I wasn't going into tryouts hoping to make the team and praying coach will give me a spot. NO!!! I just focused on dominating anyone who stood in my way, because in my eyes that spot on the team was mine -- the coach and the other players just didn't know it yet. Fear was no longer a part of my vocabulary F.E.A.R. for most people means False Evidence Appearing Real. That summer, I decided F.E.A.R. for me would be defined as Face Everything And Rise.

Many people saw the struggles that I had to battle with in life as a disadvantage. However, at this moment, I understood that nothing in life is given. You have to earn it, and I knew this from experience. In this case I was willing to fight for a spot on the team.

Now I know all this sounds good, but there comes a time in life when all the planning, preparation, and positive self-talk can't help you anymore. When it's game time, you then have to back up what you said you were going to do. Over the next two days I worked myself harder than I ever had before. I dove for every loose ball, I pushed myself through every sprint, and most of all, I dominated on the court. By the last day of the three-day tryout, a few people had already been cut from the team, and a few more would be cut before all was said and done.

If you're reading this and you have been in or are in a similar situation, where you had a goal and you were told by someone else that you were not good enough; that you tried your hardest and you still came up short; that on the first try you weren't picked for the scholarship, internship, promotion, college, or team; I want you to know this isn't a sign for you to quit or give up. This is actually a sign for you to keep working toward this goal. This is an opportunity for you to show everyone just how bad you want it. This is your chance to make believers out of the haters, doubters, and the naysayers. Because if I know only one truth, it is that it is extremely hard and nearly impossible to defeat someone who will never quit!

I knew that, for me to make the team, I had to play better than this kid who made the team the year before and who played the same position as me. In this situation you would think I was the underdog, but that wasn't the case. I had something he didn't have: "**Passion, Hunger and Drive**". I knew he had underestimated me coming into this basketball season, along with his trash talk and slick comments about me getting cut. I can admit that the year before he was a better player than me and one of the coach's favorites.

But I always believed in the saying, "Hard work beats talent if talent isn't working hard". Over the summer I knew he wouldn't put in the same effort as I did to get better as a basketball player. While he was making $500 weekly deposits into his basketball bank account, I spent the summer weeks depositing $2,000 into my account. I knew he wouldn't dedicate the same amount of time and effort to improving his game as I did because he had too many distractions. When he was sleeping, I was grinding. When he was hanging out with friends I was taking 500 jump shots. I understood that this dream I wanted was going to have to come at a sacrifice, but I was willing to pay the price. I was "ALL IN."

On the third day, I had him right where I wanted him in a battle of "Will", not "Skill". He might have played on an expensive AAU basketball team, his family might have come from privilege, but the one thing he couldn't do was "OUT WORK ME!"

There comes a time in your life when you have a goal or a dream and you have to ask yourself, "How bad do you want it?" And then you have to spend the rest of the time doing the work necessary to make your dreams into a reality. At the end of the day, I made the team and achieved my goal because

Hard work + Dedication = Success

This next level of hard work not only got me a spot on the basketball team, but, as I continued to live by the W.I.T. mentality, I was rewarded with the starting power forward spot the following year. Then I played four years of college basketball, and later became a Men's College Basketball Assistant Coach for several years. I was able to achieve all these things because I didn't believe the limitations that other people wanted to place on me. I didn't believe my own self-doubt about possibly dreaming too big. Instead, I kept faith in myself and woke up every day willing to do whatever it takes to *Live My Dreams and Not my Fears.*

Special Commentary

The question I get a lot is why didn't you transfer to a different high school team? And the truth is I was tempted, but I was raised to never run from my problems, but to face them head on. I had an uphill battle and I knew that, but being the underdog was nothing new to me. And on a more personal note, I was more upset that the coach really thought I wasn't good enough. I was driven to prove him wrong and show him and the other coaches they made a big mistake. Just remember when you're striving for a goal you will come across easy outs or good excuses for you to do what is *Easy* instead of something *Great.*

Reflection

1. Write down a dream that you failed at?

2. Write down a time that you wanted to quit on a dream but you didn't?

Chapter 11- Drive

"Greatness is not perfection,
it is persistence in the face of adversity."
– Malik Champlain

After seeing all my hard work on the basketball court pay off, I felt more alive than ever. I then started to apply my work ethic in the classroom to see how far it would take me. Prior to this, I was a below average student with not much ambition for reading and writing. For me school never came easy and this often frustrated me to the point where I didn't have the drive to try very hard. But one of the key reasons I struggled in school was due to a handful of teachers that didn't believe in me and couldn't see my potential.

I had this one teacher in high school who I felt never liked me from the first day I walked into her classroom. Almost every time I raised my hand to answer or ask a question, she would act like she didn't see my hand up or she had this look on her face as if I was bothering her with any of my question. One day, I had to ask her a question during a test. She didn't want to get up from her desk, so I asked it across the room.

For some reason I felt nervous asking the question in front of the class and I started to stutter over my words. I immediately felt embarrassed and stopped speaking. She asked me to repeat myself and that's when one of the students decided to mimic me stuttering over my words. I was glad that no one else in the class laughed, but he thought it was hilarious and started to laugh. At that point, I went from feeling embarrassed to feeling immediate rage. I jumped out my seat and started moving all the desks between us. He quickly got up and tried to hide behind the teacher's desk. I chased him around the desk, but I didn't say anything because I was so angry I thought I would start to stutter again. I felt like Arnold Schwarzenegger in "The Terminator", as I moved everything out of my way in complete anger.

Eventually, security came running and dragged me into the hallway. But before I left, I remember my teacher telling me, "You're going to be in jail by the time you're 18 years old".

This really upset me because I was trying very hard in her classroom prior to this situation. At the time, I could have admitted the situation got out of hand, but I never got in trouble in her classroom before this incident. I was so mad about her comment, but as I sat in the principal's office, I started to think, *is she right?*

This interaction with my teacher didn't help my drive to be a better student in school and it made me feel like I had more in common with the guys on the corner than my peers going to college. But with every Ying there is a Yang, and with every bad teacher there is a good one.

Later on that year, I was still holding onto a grudge with all my other teachers due to the action of one. I remember getting in trouble for talking in my history class, and my teacher Mrs. Dooley gave me a detention. By this time in school I had a reputation for not staying for detentions and instead taking Saturday detention or an in-school suspension. Things didn't change in this case, and I didn't stay for the detention.

Usually the teacher would give me a nasty look the next day, or would tell the class out loud how I had another detention. But this time things were different; she didn't say anything until I went to leave for lunch. She told me that I had to stay with her. So, I got my food and came back, for the first 2 minutes I sat there with my head on the desk like usual waiting for the next 20 minutes to slowly drag on by.

But then she started to talk to me, asking me why I didn't show up for her detention. Typically I would have ignored her and kept my head on the desk, but there was something about her voice that was sincere. I told her that my family couldn't afford a babysitter, so I had to get home every day to get my brothers off the bus. I didn't tell anyone else because I didn't want people knowing my family business or feeling sorry for us. Her response was interesting. She told me that, first, I still didn't have the right to talk while she was teaching in class. Then she told me I had another lunch detention tomorrow. This caught me by surprise. Afterward, she told me how sorry she was about my situation and then proceeded to spend the remaining time explaining to me how brilliant and full of potential I was. Back then I only remembered my mother speaking to me like that, and it felt like this teacher believed in me, when I still had questions about **Who I Was?**

The following day I stayed for my lunch detention and she spent more time asking me questions about my future -- questions that I never asked myself. *Where I was going after high school? What college would I like to attend? What will be my major? Where will I be in five years? Had I thought about taking Honors History next semester?*

My answers to all the questions were, "I don't know". But, this was exactly the spark I needed to get my brain focused on my future and where I wanted to go in life.

These two situations are perfect examples of how life and death are in the power of the tongue. I know that, during this time in my life, I wasn't perfect; but, one teacher decided to kick me when I was down and another decided to believe in me when I didn't give her much to believe in. I'm not even sure she knew how much she did for me and how much I appreciate it. So, if Lorraine Dooley is reading this book, thank you!

Reflection

- Write at least 3 people that have helped you out in your life and How did they help you?

- What's your definition of Greatness?

Chapter 12 - Soar With The Eagles

"I learned, when I look in the mirror and tell my story, that I should be myself and not peep whatever everybody is doing"
- Kendrick Lamar

Mark Twain wrote into existence my favorite quote of all time: "The two most important days in your life are the day you were born, and the day you find out why." This quote means everything to me because once you know what you're fighting, hustling, and striving for, you have a different level of DRIVE. Knowing your purpose in life allows you to see exactly what's most important to you and what's not. You start to change the people you hang out with, the environment you keep yourself in, and most of all your decision making changes.

This change started with the belief that I could actually get accepted into college and be the first in my family to do it. No disrespect to my mother, but she didn't graduate high school. My biological father and "Stepfather" both were convicted felons and didn't believe in formal education. I was choosing to be the statistical outlier because I was diagnosed with a learning disability, born with a speech impediment, and

I lived in a low income neighborhood where going to college was usually looked down upon. I remember when guys would come home from prison and they would be celebrated; but if you went to college in my neighborhood, everyone either assumed you were a sell out or you thought you were better than everyone else.

However, when I looked outside my window I knew my dreams didn't live there. I had dreams and goals bigger than being a drug dealer or a gang banger. My mother always told me, "You can't have minimum wage work ethic and have million dollar dreams". So, instead of worrying about what I didn't have, I decided to start working for everything I spent my nights praying for. I finally understood that I didn't have obligations. Instead I had the opportunity of a lifetime in front of me --the opportunity to break the cycle of self-destruction and poverty, to not be known as a follower but a "Leader". This motivation helped me turn my grades around and pushed me to make better choices in my life. However, better choices doesn't mean easier because the easy choices have always lead me down the wrong path.

At this time, I didn't know it but I was in the process of reinventing myself. I was the caterpillar slowly transforming into the butterfly. But when I was in that cocoon process no one seemed to notice the changes I made until about 3-6 months later. I'm serious; it took my teachers about 3 months to notice how much more dedicated I was to my class work, and it took my friends about 6 months before they started to say, "you changed".

The crazy part is that once my teachers noticed the change they were happy for me, I wish I could've said the same about some of my friends. Not having the support from those friends was hard for me at first until I understood that loyalty has an expiration date, just like the carton of milk I would get with my school lunch.

We didn't have much money or a lot of expensive things where I came from, so "Respect" and "Loyalty" meant everything to us. But over time, I learned that if I'm loyal to someone else or a group of people more than I am loyal to myself, I will be a fool. I've known people that got themselves in serious trouble due to "Respect" and Loyalty".

These people were getting into fights, disrespecting their parents and teachers, participating in criminal activity, and more.

However, I made the decision to use my new found success in school to see who my real friends were because they would want the best for me. This was a huge wake up call for me because, once I started separating myself from people that didn't have my best interest in mind, great things started happening for me. I made the honor roll, my SAT scores went up, and I got accepted into multiple colleges. The greatest accomplishment for me was the smile I put on my mother's face because I knew I was making her proud, and that feeling was "PRICELESS".

I believe that every person has a fire burning inside of them and that fire inspires you to chase and achieve your goals. I also have come to learn that every person's fire is a little different; some burn stronger than others, for a variety of reasons. "Dream Killers", better known as "Haters", are the number one reason many of those fires are so weak.

The "Dream Killers" see your ambition to do something great and it threatens them. In return they tell you, "It's not possible", "You could never do that", "Do yourself a favor and quit". These are all the ways people try to transfer their negative energy on to you in order to kill your dream. Over the years, I developed the term "Wood Words". Every time someone tried to break me down or tell me I wasn't good enough, I took those words and, like wood, I chopped them up and threw them into my internal fire.

I choose to not easily forget their "Wood Words", but instead I remember them and use them for added motivation to prove people wrong. My whole life I've been the underdog and had to overcome the odds, and instead of running from it, I embraced the struggle and found joy in succeeding anyways. **I want to thank all my haters for the added motivation.**

Nevertheless, three weeks before I would arrive at my first year of college I had to make a life choice that would change not just my life forever.

During my senior year in high school, I was recruited to play basketball at Western New England College. One hot summer day, I was working on my game with one of my close friends. Where I'm from, the drug dealers hang out and conduct business around the basketball courts.

After a good workout we started to walk home when one of the drug dealers in the neighborhood called us over. Now this wasn't some low-level punk – this was the dude that you had to give respect to if you wanted to walk around your neighborhood with no problems. I walked up to his car and immediately noticed it smelled like marijuana. There were two other people in the car sharing a bottle of liquor. He told me he was going to give us a ride home. It was hot that day, and I lived about a mile away from the basketball courts, never mind the peer pressure and consequences I faced if I said, "No".

Even though I was faced with this dilemma I knew that if I got into that car anything could go down and if I got in trouble it would be my fault. I had too many people counting on me and I didn't want to let them down. With this in mind I said, "Nah, I'm good." I turned around and walked away.

I wish this was where the story ended, but my friend didn't have the same resolve as I did, and he accepted the ride. To make a long story short, if I could snap shot our lives in three weeks, I was going to play ball at a four year college and he was going to play at a junior college. This was what I like to call our Drake moment, our "started from the bottom now we're here" moment, but all that came to an end for my friend.

That car ride was a lot more that a car ride and he was later arrested for being "guilty by association". There was a crime committed while he was present during a stop on that car ride home and even though he didn't participate, he also didn't notify the proper authorities. This incident led to him receiving a felony conviction and time to serve in prison. He served the next 4 years in prison, while I served the next 4 years in college. This all came from one decision and the crazy part is that, if I hopped in that car with him, I would have served that same time because back then I believed in that old street code of "No Snitching". This is why I'm telling you, loyalty to certain people should have an expiration date.

I'm telling this story to help you understand that at the end of the day life comes down to *"Choices"*. You can make four amazing choices to help you succeed in life, but one bad choice will cancel all those good choices out. I have seen this time and time again, from teen pregnancy, to DUI arrests, to stealing from a store, to cheating on a test, to writing a mean social media post, and even lying to someone who trusts you. In every situation it doesn't matter what you did in the past. At that moment, you are wrong and the consequence could adversely change your life.

I was lucky enough to get advice from my high school basketball coach, Neal Curland. He said, "Character isn't about what you do when everyone is looking, it's about what you do when you think no one is looking." This helped me understand the importance of character in myself and the people I chose to be around. Going into college, I told myself I was going to stop flying with the birds and instead I was going to start soaring with the eagles.

Reflection

- Write down a situation when you made the right decision to keep you out of trouble.

- List your 4 closest friends and why they are a good or bad influence to you.

Chapter 13- Big Ego

"Pressure can burst a pipe or pressure can make a diamond."
- Robert Horry Former NBA Player

I remember the day my mother dropped me off at college. This was the moment when I realized that she wasn't going to be there to guide me anymore. This was the moment I realized that people were counting on me to succeed and, in my mother's case, expecting it. I spent my whole life being the underdog, fighting for everything people told me I couldn't have. However, no one prepared me for the weight of high expectations and the pressure to have one shot at changing your life. I felt like when I was leaving for college everyone I knew wanted me to succeed, and for them, seeing me succeed allowed people to live vicariously through me.

I thought that representing my family, my neighborhood, and my city alone would push me to focus and dedicate myself to school work. Instead it was the total opposite. I came into college a highly recruited basketball player and I wanted to go through the full college experience.

During my first semester, I majored in partying and minored in hanging out at the campus cafeteria. I totally forgot what was most important to me and what my priorities should have been. This was my first taste of having a "BIG EGO"; all the attention I got from being this "Highly Recruited Athlete" just made it bigger and bigger. I was living for the moment not thinking about the consequences. Looking back, I know now that it was the first time in my life that I was totally selfish.

Toward the end of my first semester in college, I was already the starting power forward on the basketball team as a freshman. I believed in "playing hard, and partying hard", and this mentality left no room for school work, especially on game nights.

I remember one morning, after a big game, I walked in late to my 8 am English class that I was barely passing. The moment I stepped through the door, I saw my teammate and good friend Deon. He pointed at me and said, "Here goes Mr. Double Double", and the rest of the class laughed and I got a couple of high fives on my way to taking a seat in the back. The teacher was not impressed and she immediately asked me for my homework. I replied, "Malik Champlain doesn't do homework on game nights, I'll get that to you tomorrow!" Then I gave a small laugh and started whispering to this guy next to me.

This sounds crazy to me now, but during the time I promise you, I had a "BIG EGO". The teacher simply looked at me, said, "Ok", and went to her computer for a few minutes before proceeding to teach class. At the time, I seriously thought the teacher and I had an understanding and that she was cool with what I said.

However, as it turned out, she was not. About 15 minutes later, I saw the door swing open, and there was my basketball coach. The man that sat in my mother's living room, very nice and charismatic, but dedicated to letting my mother know he would look out for me and put me in my place if I was out of control on campus. The coach kept his promise. He stormed into the classroom, reprimanded me in front of the entire class, and had me apologize to the teacher but my retribution didn't stop there. An hour before practice, he put me through a gruesome work out that I still haven't forgotten.

Yet, the largest impact that he made on me occurred a few days after he was done being upset with me. We spoke in his office and he reminded me how bad my mother wanted me to graduate from college, the role model I was for my younger brothers, and the commitment I made to the basketball team. After that conversation, I really felt like I was letting people down due to my own selfishness, the pressure to succeed, and this new found popularity. I was lucky enough not to fail out my first semester, and I went home for a few weeks for winter break. When I came back to start the spring semester, I made a promise to myself that I would never forget the humble beginnings I came from. I would embrace the responsibility of being a leader for my family and my community. I reminded myself that I still have a lot more to prove, to accomplish, and to achieve.

Reflection

- Why is it bad to have a 'Big Ego"?

- Write down the most important people in your life.

Chapter 14- They call me "CAP"

*It matters not how strait the gate, how charged with punishments the
scroll, I am the master of my fate; I am the captain of my soul."*
—William Ernest Henley

Over the next few years, I had a big dream to win a postseason
Men's College Basketball Championship. In my dreams, it was
the NCAA Division I Tournament Championship, but I was
more than happy to be the Senior Captain of the 2007 Eastern
College Athletic Conference (ECAC) Division III Regional
Championship Team. I will live everyday for the rest of my life
with a smile on my face because "WE" won the last game of my
collegiate career. I couldn't have done it without my team, but I
also believe my team couldn't have done it without me.

On every team there are numerous pieces, kind of like a
puzzle, that have to be put together in order to create
something special. Everyone brings something different to the
game, whether it is Heart, Skill, Talent, or Humor. During my
senior year, my team had all the pieces, but that wasn't good
enough. There had to be someone wise enough to put these
pieces in the right places, someone with experience, and

someone who understands how to build a winning culture. This person was our new head coach, Mike Theulen.

Coach Theulen had a vision when he first took over the team during my second year of college. I remember once he looked me in the eyes and said, "Your legacy as a basketball player will only be carried on by your teammates in that locker room. This will be your team soon, so tell me how do you want to be remembered?"

I remember looking at the ceiling in my dorm room asking myself, "How do I want to be remembered?", and I remember thinking that I didn't want to be easily forgotten, I wanted to leave a lasting legacy. This question would stick with me for the next two seasons. At the end of my third year in college the question still remained, "What will I do when it's my turn, my team?"

Throughout my basketball career I had many captains. I started thinking back to my junior year in high school; we had a great team that year and I was just happy to be on the varsity team getting whatever minutes I could. We lost the conference regular season title by losing in 3 out of our last 4 games. This was very disappointing for the team, who had so much to live up to after going to the state championship game the year before.

The following week of practice, this was the week

leading into the playoffs, I didn't know what to expect from the head coach because he was frustrated with how bad we were playing and the team just couldn't buy a win. However, I remember our senior captain, Kenny Jones, wouldn't give up on the season, and especially not the team.

During practice, no one pushed themselves harder than Kenny, he would do push ups after any free throw shot he missed, and if he turned the ball over during a scrimmage he would get on the line and start running sprints. Soon enough the whole team was doing push ups and running sprints with him. He really helped me with my confidence. If he saw me put my head down after a bad play, he would yell, "Keep your head up!" He always reminded me, "As long as you're wearing that jersey you wear that red and white with pride". Kenny's will to win, and his inner drive to not let us fail, helped push us to victory.

Now, Kenny wasn't the only good basketball player we had on that team, but I know for every sprint we ran in practice, for every push up we did, for every minute we played in those games, we did it for him. It was his senior year and we knew how much he sacrificed, how much he wanted it. At the end of the day, we just never wanted to let him down.

Why is this important? Fast forward four years later, and picture that awkward, lanky forward, the one that sat at the end of the bench, now being referred to as the most endearing name any player on a team can have: "Captain".

I quickly learned that college was all about building relationships with your peers and the professors that help teach, mentor and guide you. This realization helped me develop a relationship with every member on the team going into my senior year, especially the two seniors Peter and Deon. There is something about going through shared experiences with people that helps grow a strong relationship. I spent three years, day in and day out, with these two, sacrificing and pushing each other to get to our senior season.

As a Captain on this team, I would refer to the word "Family" a lot to describe our togetherness. And like most families we argued and fought at times, but most of all we had each other's' backs, especially if someone from outside the "Family" messed with one of the members. It was the strength in character that was built in me, that family was everything. My teammates were like my little brothers, so I took care of them,

I will always remember playing for Coach Theulen and being part of a team with 12 of my closest friends. That year, we did what many people didn't think we were capable of, and that sacrificing the "Me" for "We" and the word "Team" for "Family". My coach once asked, "What will I do when it's my team? How will I be remembered?" When it was my turn, I did it by believing in something that was bigger than me. I decided to walk by faith and not by sight and I was blessed because of it.

Reflection

- List the characteristics of a leader.

- What does it mean to "walk by faith and not by sight?"

Chapter 15- Live Your Dreams

"They say anything's possible. You gotta dream like you never seen obstacles"

- J. Cole

If I had any advice it would be to "Dream Big!!" I mean dream as if there are no ceilings, no limits, and no fear. Once I stopped caring about what other people thought about me and just focused all my energy into just being my best version, my whole life changed. When I first got to college, the truth was I felt like I didn't belong. When I looked around the campus, there were only a handful of students or faculty that looked liked me. I wasn't top of my class or in the honors society in high school like a lot of my peers. I was even taking a remedial English course, which made me feel unprepared to be in college.

In the midst of my meltdown, a lunch lady whose name I later found out was "Ms. Brenda" would always check in with me whenever she saw me. Ms. Brenda was the type of person that just made you feel at home, especially when she referred to you as "Baby". In the winter when it was cold outside, she would ask if you had a coat. If you stayed around campus for the summer, she always made it a point to ask if you needed a home cooked meal. I don't believe Ms. Brenda obtained a higher education degree, but she definitely had her Master's in hospitality and had her PhD in getting people to open up to her.

One day, I was just having a hard time with school. I felt homesick, and was tired of the early morning classes and late night practices. I was sitting in the cafeteria by myself for a few minutes after it had closed. She must have noticed me because she came over and sat down next to me. I remember just telling her everything I was thinking for the next fifteen minutes. When I was finished, I could tell from the look on her face that she must have been cut from the same cloth as my mother, because she wasn't feeling sorry for me. She looked me in my eyes and said, "I once heard this quote "First they will ignore, then they will laugh at you, then they will fight you, but then you win!" Then she said, "You remember that baby, you just gotta hold on because your day to win is coming."

That was the best advice for me at that moment because, as I thought about what she said, I understood that has been happening to me my whole life: when my mother had me as a teenager, when I first said I wanted to go to college, even when I got cut from the basketball team.

The whole time people thought they could predict my success, that they could guarantee I was going to be another P.O.M.E. (product of my environment). Frank Sinatra has a quote, "The best revenge is massive success." It was this type of guidance that I received in college along with the every other day calls from my mother that helped push me to graduate with my Bachelor's degree. I would later receive my Master's degree from Sacred Heart University a few years later.

I'm living proof that it doesn't matter what people call you, only what you answer to. If you have dreams and goals, you have to fight for them because people will see you doing what they told themselves they couldn't do and try to sabotage your success. Here is a fact: it will not be easy chasing your dreams. But the silver lining is that anyone who has achieved a dream will tell you it is 100% worth it. The long days, sleepless nights, early mornings, all the time you invest into your dream versus time spent being unproductive.

The road to making your dreams a reality is not easy, but the easy road only leads to regret. One day it will be your turn to make that tough decision to follow the crowd or follow your dreams. On that day I want you to ask yourself this question: *"Do you want it Easy or Do you want it Great?"*

And since I know everyone reading this book wants it

Great! I want you to speak these words into existence:

I have Passion, I have Hunger, I have Drive;

I am Powerful, I am Fearless, I am Unstoppable,

I am Alive, I am Amazing, I am a Champion,

I am Strong.

I will live my Dreams and Face my FEARS!

Repeat 2x or until you believe it!!!

Chapter 16 - Epilogue

In that moment, I heard the gunshots. I closed my eyes and I just prayed that I wasn't shot. When I opened them I felt all over my body for a gun wound and I didn't have one. Someone else in the crowd shot into the air and everyone scattered, running in different directions. In that moment, I yelled for my friend Dee, "Come on, and hop in the car". As soon as Dee got into the car we drove off down the street.

It took less than a minute before we saw a police car on the other side of the street turn on their lights, switch into our lane and pull us over. At this point the front of the police cruiser is pointing at the front of our car and they had those bright police lights blinding our sight. I'm not going to lie; I tried to stay strong, but I had tears running down my cheeks because I knew everything I ever worked for was going to be wasted. The lights felt like they were on us for like five minutes, but it lasted more like 30 seconds. But the police officers never got out the car. They simply reversed and drove off like they had something more important to handle.

I bring up this story to show you how one bad decision when I was 16 years old could have ruined my life. If I got shot and was killed how many people would that affect besides just me? If I had been arrested, what would have happened to my dreams of playing college basketball and earning my degree? Would I have the same influence to get my younger brothers to follow my footsteps and go to college?

I was placed in a really bad situation, and I got lucky. But the good decisions I made in the future made me even luckier in life. Do yourself the favor, and think before you do. Think about how your actions influence and affect others, especially the people you love and even the people you don't know are looking up to you.

In conclusion, I wish you Health, Wealth, and Everything this world has to offer. You are more than a Conqueror. You are built to win. Fear has no control over your life. Grind until your dreams are a reality and most of all *Live Your Dreams, Not Your Fears.*

ABOUT THE AUTHOR

Renowned speaker Malik Champlain's message is both forceful and inspiring because of his ability to connect and encourage people to strive for more. He was recently named one of the 100 Men of Color in Connecticut and also honored by the NAACP with their Martin Luther King Legacy Award. Malik's energizing narrative includes his journey from being raised in poverty, labeled a special education student, and living out of his car. However, Malik's story doesn't end there; he has risen to become a Motivational Speaker, Author, Entrepreneur, Social Activist, Former Men's College Basketball Head Assistant Coach, and more.

Contact information:
- Email: Malikchamplain@gmail.com
- Website: www.passionhungerdrive.com
- Facebook- Public Figure Page: Malik Champlain

Made in the USA
Charleston, SC
07 February 2017